LIBER TAO

LIBER TAO

One Man's View of The Way

BY T.C. EISELE

REBEL SATORI PRESS
New Orleans

Book Design: Sven Davisson
Cover Photo:

ISBN: 978-1-60864-115-4

Rebel Satori Press
www.rebelsatoripress.com

To

The Old Master

Within us all

&
For
Diana

INTRODUCTION

This book is a love child born from the mingling of the Mystical Traditions of both the West and the East. To illustrate its mixed heritage I have chosen to title this work "Liber Tao," a pairing of the Latin word Liber or "Book" with the Chinese word Tao or "The Way" whose combined translation, "The Book of the Way," is a direct reference to the legendary classic of Chinese Mysticism known as the "Tao-Te Ching."

It has been my intention with "Liber Tao" to recreate my own version of the "Tao-Te-Ching." By "my own version" I do not mean another translation or interpretation of the original masterwork, but rather a brand new effort based on the experiences and insights I have gained while trying to forge my own "Way" in life. In homage to the great Chinese classic I have subsequently organized this current work into the same format and style as the original "Tao-Te-Ching," namely a collection of 81 entries (none longer than a single page) with each one written in a direct, minimal fashion.

Many of the viewpoints I share in "Liber Tao" have been drawn from my work as a Professional Astrologer and Psychic Counselor in New York City over the last 15 years. During that time I was also involved in a serious study of the Practical Qabalah, otherwise known as Ritual Magick or "the Yoga of the West." After years of performing my Occult exercises, I found that my ability to comprehend what I read in the Tao-Te-Ching began to increase. In fact, as I gained more of a holistic understanding of the Tao I also began to feel less of a need to engage in Ritual Work, exchanging it for a quieter, Eastern style of meditation. From this new form of daily spiritual practice I began to explore the Tao as the source from which all consciousness emanates. I believe this view represents my spiritual maturity and from it I have found the impetus to write "Liber Tao."

Of course the cheekiness of writing my own Tao will no doubt raise some eyebrows, yet shouldn't the purpose of spiritual study be not only to accept and honor tradition, but also to keep tradition vital and alive by adding something to it from our own experience? At this point I owe a nod to the American Artist and Cartoonist R. Crumb, for it was only after seeing his illustrated version of the Bible that I said to myself, "Why not?" in regards to writing my own Tao.

Now that the deed has been done, I can only hope "Liber Tao" will be seen as a sincere effort rather than just an exercise of ego. Perhaps like "The Fool" of the Tarot I am walking off a cliff and whether I fall or fly will be revealed in due time. Meanwhile, for those of you who are unfamiliar with the "Tao-Te-Ching," let me take a moment to provide some essential background on the great Chinese Classic that has provided the inspiration for this current work.

Considered by many to be one of the eminent spiritual books of the world, The "Tao-Te-Ching" of Ancient China is the seminal text of a philosophical and spiritual system known as "Taoism." When translated directly from Chinese into English, the meanings of the words Tao, Te, and Ching forming the title of this great classic are respectively, "Way", "Virtue", and "Book", so that all together "Tao-Te-Ching" literally means " The Book of the Virtuous Way". Often referred to as simply, "The Tao," this remarkable work has been the object of numerous translations as well as extensive commentary and analysis. I first became aware of "The Tao" more than twenty years ago and during that time have consulted its ageless wisdom over and over again.

By itself, the term "Tao" represents an idea that is at the center of all Chinese thought. While its most common translation is " The Way," conceptually the Tao may also be thought to mean a path, a method, a principle, a doctrine, or even the matrix of universal consciousness. Yet beyond all these possible translations, the Tao is ultimately recognized by the Chinese mind to be the symbolic name for the eternal essence from which all other reality emanates.

Even though it is believed that the true nature of the Tao is beyond human comprehension, ancient Taoists nevertheless endeavored to find traces of the Way in nature, the social world, and also within the individual. As a result, the Chinese feel there is a Tao or Way that represents the purest and most truthful approach to any activity or form of being. The desire to be more in touch with this type of awareness is essentially the driving force behind all evolution, so when the Chinese speak of understanding the Tao, they are essentially referring to the possible bridge that can be forged between our normal daily perceptions and the Intuitive, Divine presence that permeates all life.

The authorship of the "Tao-Te-Ching" is commonly attributed to an individual known as Lao-Tzu, although it should be realized that when this name is translated from the Chinese the word Lao literally means "Old" and Tzu means "Master", so that this source work of Taoist Philosophy is essentially being presented as the wisdom of a generic "Old Master." With this in mind, it would not be inaccurate to think of the "Tao-Te-Ching" as being similar to the Christian Bible and its Gospels, in other words, a cultural document written by multiple individuals over a long period of time rather than being the work of any single person.

Constructed as a sequence of aphorisms, poems, and proverbs, the actual manuscript of the "Tao-Te-Ching" is a collection of 81 short entries divided into two sections, one entitled Tao or "The Way" and the other called Te or "Virtue". While the overall theme of the book is concerned with exploring how the Tao or "The Way" is at the root of all life, the section entitled Te or "Virtue" refers to the manner in which every individual being should aspire to its highest nature within the Tao. Thus the "Way of Virtue", or reflexively, "The Virtuous Way" becomes about the relationships between the Tao and its evolving individual components.

Some other important terms within the text of the "Tao-Te-Ching" that might need to be interpreted for the Western sensibility include, "Heaven and Earth," or the actual physical universe, "The Ten Thousand Things" or the endless varieties of matter that inhabit the universe, "Non-action" or the ability to let the Tao guide us beyond mere doing and into the nature of being, and "Non-existence" or the potential we can learn to sense behind the actuality of material things. It is from this last notion of "non-existence" that the Tao gains its mysterious reputation due to its seeming invisibility if one tries to isolate or define it.

Because the Chinese believe all things originate in the Tao, for the purposes of analogy it could also be thought of as a symbolic womb where all potential exists before anything is actually formed. It is from this womb that all life emerges like an embryo, thus the Tao can be compared to a Great Mother that gives birth to everything we know.

The idea of a ubiquitous energy that emanates from a causeless cause and then serves to nurture the development of all reality is not a concept exclusive to Taoism or even Eastern Spiritual Philosophy. In fact, my original understanding of this idea really owes to having first heard a very similar theory explained several years before when I began my study of the Practical

Qabalah. The Hebrew version of this idea is referred to as "The Great Egg" and is illustrated through the use of a diagram containing three concentric circles. The largest or outermost circle of this diagram is labeled AIN or "Nothingness," the next smallest one is known as AIN Soph or "The Limitless," and the innermost circle is called AIN Soph AUR or "The Limitless Light."

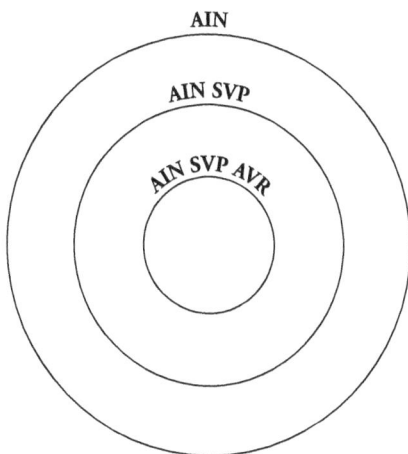

The simplest explanation of this idea would be that from the outermost circle or "Nothingness," a point of view or the "Limitless" is born. From the Limitless in turn comes "The Limitless Light," whereby the void is given form by this light and its resulting shadow. The relevancy of this to Taoist Philosophy becomes apparent if one considers the circular shape of the Taoist Unity symbol with its divisions of Yang and Yin.

The White or "Yang" half that symbolizes the masculine or "active" power and the Black or "Yin" half that symbolizes the feminine or "receptive" power would correspond to AIN Soph AUR or "The Limitless Light" and its shadow. The joining together of these halves would symbolize the Taoist notion of "Mind" and represent AIN Soph or "The Limitless," which would then serve as an intermediary to AIN or the "Nothingness" that would correspond to the ubiquitous and eternal nature of the Tao.

Much of what is expressed in the 81 entries that occupy the coming pages are reflections on what Mystics of the Western Tradition would refer to as "The Great Work," or the aspiration of the individual toward communion with a higher form of being. I do not profess to be enlightened (what truly enlightened person would?) nor do I expect everyone to agree with my observations. If I have managed to express anything profound then perhaps I really was conscious of the Tao for a moment, at least I'd like to think so. Ultimately I only hope that what I have written will motivate others to seek additional insight into their own circumstances.

Just as a computer hacker might install a virus that will manifest his or her message by first disrupting and then rearranging a program that is running on your PC, so too should "Liber Tao" be looked upon as a form of hack into the software within the human mind that maintains what the 20th Century Mystic G.I. Gurdjieff called, "modern man's sleepwalking through life."

As a result, it is entirely part of the plan if some of the ideas you are about to read don't float but instead sink like stones in the pond of your current belief system. On the other hand, if you are at least able to hear the "plunk" of what has been tossed upon the surface of your awareness, then I trust you will follow the ensuing ripples to whatever form of the truth you need to discover.

Jersey City 2014

LIBER
TAO

1

This is a book about the Tao (or the Way)
But what is the Way?

The Way comes from nothing and ends nowhere
Yet it always leads to the truth

The Way cannot be plotted nor its distance measured
Yet its bearings always feel correct

The Way appears on no globe or map
Yet it connects all people and places

Both circuitous and direct
Neither timely nor tardy
The Way is always right on schedule

Therefore, when a person has the Way
All life springs from a harmony of being

And when a person lacks the Way
Attainment only leads back to desire

2

The Way is always clear and flowing
It is only we who are muddled and stagnant

If you let muddy water sit
Its cloudiness will settle

We must release our convictions
Of the world being this or that

So we may see the clarity of the Way
And not just the muddiness of our mind

3

All movement is the movement of the mind
Likewise, all stillness is the stillness of the mind

Any change then from movement to stillness
And back again is merely another state of mind

Therefore, it is possible for the mind to encompass
    both
Movement in stillness and stillness in movement

This would explain why time seems relative
Yet eternity is absolute

As well as why we can believe so explicitly
In the realities of what we think

Without fully knowing
What the mind really is

4

We may know the conditions of the mind
But we will never know its essence

The essence of the mind is the One and the Infinite
Yet it can also be said to possesses four conditions

The first two are waking and sleep,
Which are both necessary

Waking is for the conscious maintenance of bodily
    needs
And sleep is for rest and health

Next there is sleeping while awake and waking in sleep,
Each being relative to freedom

Sleeping while awake is the total immersion in our
    body
And waking in sleep is transcending the limits of our
    body

Most people are sleeping while awake
With their mind imprisoned in their physical awareness

It is the work of an Adept to fully awaken from such
    sleep
In order to see clearly in the night of becoming

And recognize his or her connection to the Tao
Is like the full moon reflected in every body of water.

5

To observe the mind is a tricky business
We should begin by questioning what we think

Then we can come to realize how much of what we
        believe
Is merely what we've been taught

And how the notion we have of self
Is who we have learned to be.

Next we must analyze our desires
And the things we think we need

To face the inevitable challenge
Of sitting in the vacuum of self

Without suffocating
In the atmosphere of our own presence

6

The usefulness of a vessel is not how much it can hold
But rather how much it serves

This distinction is subtle, yet forms the root
Of the difference between fear and courage

Fear wants the vessel to always be full
And will hoard in anticipated need

Courage uses the vessel with impunity
Seeing the cycles of emptiness as the way of life

This dynamic is the root of all creativity
And allows the student to see how letting go

Is the first step to acquiring what is necessary

7

Necessity in life takes two forms;
What we need to survive and what we need to thrive

Survival is what must be done, yet thriving is our
    choice
This marks the real difference between animals and
    humans

Animals have a biological imperative
While humans entertain notions of desire

Animals have only one nature
Yet humans indulge an inner debate

We think this difference in perception
Makes us superior to the animals

Yet if our self importance threatens the greater
    environment
Then our nature has fallen below that of the animals

This is the first step in realizing the difference
Between the high and the low within ourselves.

8

Understanding the higher and lower aspects in our
    nature
Is necessary for our evolution

On one level, a view from higher ground will allow
A perspective of the world beyond ourselves

On another level, going within the self allows for
A view of life beyond the physical environment

Therefore, to an evolved individual
The meaning of high or low

Is relevant to what the ego recognizes
As the parameters of the self

9

The Center and the perimeter of a circle
Are like the self and the world

We can infer one from the other
But from which does reality originate?

This is the paradox of consciousness in the universe

生

BIRTH

10

Consciousness is a tincture
Containing time and space-

Like an ocean rocking
Between beach and sky

Eroding one
And evaporating into the other-

A homogeneous solvent
And heterogeneous solution

Comprising the amniotic fluid for all things

11

Is vision real because I observe something?
Or because I am observed?

If the mind doesn't stir inside
The world doesn't arise outside

Therefore vision becomes real
When the mind and the World are transparent

12

The nature of our being is threefold;
The mind, the body, and the spirit

The nature of our environment is also threefold;
Affirmation, denial, and reconciliation

The nature of how being and environment interact
Is threefold as well; life, death, and eternity

These nine principles,
Beginning and ending in nothing,

Are the decimal system used
To form the equations of existence

13

The universe is perfect
Because everything in it fits

Accordingly, no single thing can be perfect
If it is removed from the whole

Perfection then needs to be understood
As a precise harmony of interaction

In the absence of which,
Nothing can fulfill its destiny

14

Only two types of interactions
Are possible in the universe;

To Analyze or synthesize-
To divide or unite

If something is to be changed it must either be
Split into parts or something else added

Yet neither of these processes
Taken to their extremes

Can either dilute or complete
The **A**bsolute **O**rder

15

In trying to resist change

We are longing for a state
That would have to be motionless

Yet if this was possible
Where would we be?

And after such a discovery
Would we still be the same?

16

The Tao, the Qabalah, various Yogas and Rituals,
These are all holistic approaches to the truth

Career, possessions, power, and control,
These are all selfish approaches to the truth

No matter which approach you use,
The truth will always result;

You will get what you deserve

17

What makes a true Master?

If humility is important
He will be inconspicuous

If patience is important
He will be willing to wait

If respect is important
He will treat you as equal

If kindness is important
He will make you feel safe

If he is open, he will let himself be led
If he is strong, he will let himself be vulnerable

If he is wise, he will be open to others
If he is truthful, he won't try to convince

But most important of all,
If you are none of these things

He will not presume
You should be different

18

Amidst all your thinking
What are you not considering?

A problem cannot be solved
With the same mindset that created it

So what are you willing
To let transform you?

Without the unknown
Creativity is impossible

Therefore, at some point
Whatever you don't know

Will be what offers the space
For whatever you really need.

死

DEATH

19

Psychic abilities are of the mind
Enlightenment is of the Tao

The mind is a reference point and therefore finite
The Tao is nothing and therefore infinite

A psychic perceives the mysteries of existence
Enlightenment experiences the truth of non-existence

The mind is thought and thought is attachment
The Tao is without thought and therefore non-
    attachment

A psychic is aware of being psychic
An Enlightened Consciousness holds no distinctions

20

What is the meaning of non-action,
And how is it possible?

Most people think
Non-action means doing nothing

Imagine an orchestra playing music,
During any solo the other musicians stop playing

Can we say these musicians are doing nothing
If the orchestra is performing a piece of music?

Non-action therefore means
To allow for the spaces the universe provides

So this composition called "Life"
Can unfold in perfect time

21

If non-action is about timing
Then action is about content

Not merely the degree or technique of an act
But the essence within us where the will to act is born

Any action we perform
Must have a sense of being that precedes it

Having this sense in its proper place
Describes the adept who has struggled with himself

The nature of this struggle entails
Confronting the negative thoughts we habitually
    manufacture

What is meant by negative thoughts?
Compulsive mental activity removing us from the
    present

Much of our normal behavior falls into this category
Which is why modern life is so high on stress

And low on fulfillment

22

There are two ways to learn the truth
About the relative value of things

The first is not getting what you want
And the other is getting what you want

In not getting what you want
You will remain separate from the object of your desire

In getting what you want, the object of your desire
Will still be something separate from you

Recognizing this will mean you are ready
To hear about the Tao

23

The notion of the Tao
Is vague to the skeptic
Yet clear for the mystic

The substance of the Tao
Is fantastic to the skeptic
Yet real for the mystic

The mysteries of the Tao
Are resisted by the skeptic
Yet accepted by the mystic

Vagueness and clarity
Fantasy and reality
To resist or accept

The lessons of the Tao
Are the same for everyone

24

If the mind is the builder
Then what is the Tao?

The mind builds from what is known
This is why our problems often follow patterns

Solutions must therefore come from the unknown
This is why creativity sometimes seems unconscious

The mind cannot build the unknown
But instead must let the unknown be the builder

From this we can begin to sense a connection
Between the mind and the Tao

25

When the mind is divided by what it sees
People are drawn into illusions of empty or full

In a mind that is uninterrupted, empty is not missing
    anything
And full does not attach to anything

Therefore, when there is no discrimination between
    things
The mind ceases to be divided against itself with desire

To see the world for what it is with the mind undivided
Is to be aware of the immediate presence of the Tao

Thus when the surface of the pond is without ripples
The Tao is the mind and the mind is the Tao

26

We fear being vulnerable
Yet suffer separateness

We hide our feelings
Then long to be understood

We want what is fair
But always on our terms

We yearn for relationships
Yet shy away from responsibility

This is the constant inner struggle for any seeker
Like hot and cold fronts creating a thunderstorm

And then, lightning!

27

Whatever we think we want
Is because we feel unfulfilled

Therefore, by not longing for anything
We accept the present as fulfilling

As a result, the mastery of our desire
Is more efficient than acquiring a fortune

WOMAN

28

There is no back door to enlightenment
There is no front door either

There are no windows to peek in
For there is no structure to house it

There is no single path to enlightenment
For it encompasses all paths

There is no partial enlightenment
Just as a woman can't be half pregnant

No one can give you enlightenment
Or even prepare you for it

As a result, speaking of enlightenment
Is like trying to explain sex to a virgin

When the time is right
Everything occurs naturally

And then one knows

29

Great wisdom resides
In a half glass of water

If you are very thirsty
More water is needed

If you are not thirsty
There is water for later

To say the glass is half full
Is to increase ourselves and reduce the world

To say the glass is half empty
Is to reduce ourselves and increase our fear

Therefore, we must first accept the world as it is
Before we can quench our thirst for the truth

30

The person who does not know
Will try to stop the world
So they may hold perfection

The person who knows
Will let the world go
So perfection may hold them

31

What is the true nature of power?

Collective power is the perfect harmony of all things
Individual power is cooperating with this perfection

The power of heaven is the activeness in all things
The power of earth is the receptiveness in all things

The power of being creates the causes of all things
The power of doing creates the existence of all things

Thus the true nature of power is equilibrium

Between the collective and the individual,
Heaven and earth, being and doing

32

The mind is logical
And the spirit is intuitive

Hence the mind will pursue the idea of love
While for the spirit, love unfolds as a mystery

An idea of love can only be a limitation
Yet embracing a mystery leads to creativity

Therefore the mind can only love
Until it has a reason to hate

Yet the spirit continuously loves
Through its unfolding creative nature

Hate then is a mechanism of the mind
While love is a manifestation of the spirit

And the Tao is their eternal, bittersweet romance.

33

What are the true natures of the known and the
    unknown?

The true nature of the known is limitation
And the true nature of the unknown is an open mind

This explains how we can possess our consciousness
Without actually knowing what it is

34

Can there be meaning
Without meaninglessness?

When there are no distinctions
There is nothing

Yet can nothing exist?
And, if so, could it then also not exist?

Can there be distinctions
And no distinctions at the same time?

This is why it can be said of the Tao
That it is conspicuous in its seeming absence

35

The Tao is not elusive
We are just lost in its reflections

The Tao is not a master plan
We are just obsessed with having one

The Tao is not chaos
Like our fear of the unknown

The Tao is also not harmony
Like our hopes to be safe and sound

Thus it is difficult to speak of the Tao
Without limiting it

It is difficult to seek the Tao
Without making it harder to find

It is also difficult to accept the Tao
If we expect to acquire something

Perhaps we should just agree
To let ourselves be with the Tao

Like we do with the air we breathe

36

From where do our thoughts originate?

How many ideas have we actually been taught,
All the while thinking them our own?

If we are merely part of a matrix
Of what to think, are we thinking?

One way to test our thoughtfulness
Is to form an antithesis for anything we believe

It is better if we are playful in our line of reasoning
That way we can begin to see

How much of conventional logic
Is really about emotional manipulation

Familiar equals safe
And conformity equals approval

From this we can realize
How many of our thoughts originate from fear

男

MAN

37

We decorate the walls of our minds
With ideas and images

So we can feel safe and in control
Never realizing that without these walls

We would have no fears

38

We are only limited in life
By our bodies and our minds

Hence we never suspect our desires
To be the bricks we are using to build our prison

Until a little bird perches for a moment
Between the bars covering the window

And its unexpected presence
Makes us long to see outside

39

To rebel is to give your power away
To prove you can take it back

An adept does not rebel, instead
He exercises his power by keeping it

Therefore, when faced with adversity
True strength can be still

While weakness feels the need to act

40

If the Tao encompasses both being and non-being,
The positive and the negative, the high and the low,

Then whenever we seek to find the truth
We are also asking for a lie to teach us

41

There are two types of teachers
Those who tell and those who challenge

There are two types of teachings
Those promoting rules and those promoting
    realizations

There are also two types of students
Those who imitate and those who question

Do not trust a teacher
Who requires you to be an echo

Do not trust a teaching
That is condescending toward other teachings

And do not take pride in being a student
If you only seek knowledge

But not the experience of your lessons

42

What does it mean to have a teacher
Unless one is truly a student?

What does it mean to be in the army
Unless one is truly a soldier?

What does it mean to be married
Unless one is truly a partner?

Likewise, one may faithfully obey the laws of men
Yet still not be in harmony with the Tao

43

When small children are brought to cemeteries
They want to run and play between the headstones

Yet they are scolded and told to respect
Something they do not understand

When small children are brought to churches
The candles, shadows, and echoes, seem like a funhouse

Yet they are scolded and told to respect
Something they do not understand

This is how we all get divided from the Tao
Into the illusory world of this and that

Yet there is room in a cemetery for more than death,
After all, a cemetery is maintained by the living

And there is room in a church for more than piety,
After all, a church is a refuge for the wayward in spirit

Therefore, to reunite ourselves with the Tao
We must remember to sometimes forget

All we've been taught to understand

44

Both prideful ignorance
And the ruthless pursuit of enlightenment

Will each come to judge
Something to their detriment

45

Why is forgiveness necessary
If all things are as they should be?

We must forgive ourselves
For thinking otherwise

This is how pain and suffering
Transform into evolution

変

DARKNESS

46

Science is really an exploration of the mind
Not of existence

Taoism is really an exploration of being
Not of the mind

Existence, mind, being;
Everything that is known has its limits.

Just as the atmosphere rarifies
When one climbs toward a mountaintop,

So to on the journey between mind and being
There exists a threshold of human consciousness.

It is the way of acceptance that brings us there
And the way of creativity that extends beyond

Knowledge is simply an urge
To keep looking over our shoulder

47

One of our great illusions
Is the idea of waiting

After all, is it really possible to wait
In a constantly moving universe?

In reality all being consists
Of perpetual motions crossing paths.

Therefore, what we mistake for waiting
Is just impatience with where we are.

Thus to live fully would be to accept the flow of things
And then synchronize ourselves accordingly

This is the heavenly view of time
And the standard by which the clock of the Tao
    operates

48

When a hawk lands in a tree
The smaller birds flee their perches

When the sun rises in the east
The stars depart like last night's wine

When a cloudy sky erupts with thunder
The people below start running for cover

Such is the movement of the Tao
As every moment finds its way

49

The infinite seems to be invisible
In the face of our finite attention span

This is how the Tao is able to hide
In plain sight before our very eyes

Perhaps this is because we are hoping for stability
In a world where the only constant thing is change

Thus forcing our natural evolution
Into a necessary evacuation

From what we think we know
To what we must discover

50

When we perceive the world
Without intending to do so

Like a mirror that reflects
Everything it faces

This is called "no mind"

What we think of as "mind"
Is because we discriminate

Between ourselves
And what is around us

This is why the mind is always in conflict
With the world in which it exists

Therefore, just as a mirror can be useful
For expanding the sense of a small room

So too can embracing "no mind" be of use
As a doorway beyond our discrimination

And into the Tao

51

In order to truly perceive life as it is,
Consciousness must be a communion not a point of
    view

Just as our eyes naturally work in unison
So we will not see double

So too must the mind work with no-mind
So we may see beyond our identification with things

When the known and the unknown are in conflict
All negotiations end with something dying

When the known and the unknown are in harmony
Everything becomes the Tao

52

When a cat or a dog
Chases their own tail
We are amused

Yet if someone tells us
By doing something or going someplace
They hope to find themselves

We listen with a straight face

53

In a world filled with things
What does it mean to experience emptiness?

First realize, to experience emptiness
Does not require us to eliminate anything

To experience emptiness means to be liberated
From having emotional attachments to things

Such experience does not exclude the material world
But instead allows for a more clear view of it

Thus by calmly accepting things as they truly are
Instead of indulging how we feel about them

We can begin to appreciate
The important distinction

Between reality and ego.

54

When humans created their Gods
They imagined beings that could run like a horse

Had the strength of a bear
Or could soar like an eagle

Yet when has the possession of great speed
Made a horse more than a horse?

When has great strength
Made a bear more than a bear?

Or the ability to fly
Distinguished one eagle from another?

When we imagine the powers of Gods
We are merely lamenting the reality of ourselves

For no amount of speed can escape what is real
No amount of strength can overpower what is real

And there is nowhere to soar higher than the real
Thus to understand what is real

Is the consciousness of God.

LIGHT

55

The Tao does not exist
As we would understand existence-
Bounded by birth and death

The Tao is not the truth
As we would understand the truth-
Determined by right and wrong

The Tao is not intelligence
As we would understand intelligence-
Limited by a point of view

So how can we know
The way of the Tao
When it is beyond our understanding?

In the same way as a caterpillar
Who cannot fathom itself a butterfly,

Yet something in the creature
Guides its transformation

56

If we try to measure out life
As if we are building a container

The edges of birth and death
Will never sit flush to one another

57

If you can feel the connection
Between mind and breath

Then what divides you from the world
Will open like the wings of a hawk

And you can glide toward the Sun
On currents of endless Tao

58

The true nature of stillness

Neither waits nor anticipates
Neither flows nor is stagnant

Neither infuses nor separates
Neither advances nor recedes

Like a circle
With no beginning or end

It both leaves and arrives
Surrounding and surrounded by

Birth
And Death

Thus the true nature of stillness
Is the union of all natures

59

The nature of the Tao
Derives from harmony rather than consistency

Thus allowing for both
The traditionalist and the revolutionary

To discover what is real

60

Creativity is how we interact with the unknown
The Tao is how the unknown interacts with us

Thus our consciousness is an alchemical marriage
Of an awareness of form and a formless awareness

When one does not allow this partnership to
    deteriorate
Through attachment to temporary conditions

This is known as relinquishing the mind
Without abandoning it

61

Listen to the birds at dawn
If their chorus sounds like hope
Then you have heard the Tao

Sit with the cicadas in the afternoon
If the rattling seems to keep the rhythm of the heat
Then you have felt the Tao

Watch the fireflies in the evening
If their flickering dance seems like friends bidding
	goodnight
Then you have seen the Tao

Now surrender to the end of the day
If reclining is peaceful and the darkness a caress
And if you find your mind is void of nothing more
	than this

Let consciousness close
Like the door of a tomb
Then swim in this dream like a sperm to the womb

Where the Tao is born and the Tao is you.

62

The Tao allows for every possibility
Yet the mind seeks perfection

Eternity is endless
Yet the mind searches for conclusions

Birth and death are infinitely recurring
Yet the mind forms a sequence

Being and Non-being require each other
Yet the mind retains a preference

It therefore makes perfect sense
Why museums preserve the brains of famous men in
    jars

It is a way for us to see
The nature of our limitations

63

The sky would seem to be without form or substance
Yet its form is endless and its substance ubiquitous

A thought would also seem to be without form or
    substance
Yet its form is infinite and its substance subtle

The Tao presents a different sort of mystery
As its form exists all around us

Yet its substance can only be ours.

EARTH

64

A conscious action will change our thinking more
    profoundly
Than a conscious thought will change our actions

This is the difference between
Creating a reality or inheriting one

From this subtle distinction
Truth or illusion are defined

And freedom or slavery is determined

65

There are 7 steps
Leading to the Adytum
Of Higher Consciousness

The first is emotion
Because all experience
Begins with the visceral

The second is intellect
Or processing emotion
After an experience

The third is intuition
Or sensing beyond
Either emotion or intellect

The fourth is clarity
Or when emotion and intellect
Are reconciled into being

The fifth is understanding
Meaning to know a lot
You only need to know a little

The sixth is wisdom
Meaning to know a little
You really need to know a lot

And the last is to simply sit still
And realize you have never left the Temple.

66

By acting
We acknowledge
What we need

By not acting
We acknowledge
What we have

Yet how do we acknowledge being?
By needing something
Or having something?

The Tao would tell us
It is neither

67

What are we
If not ourselves?

The self creates a point of view
That separates us from the rest of the Universe

From this isolation we then try to reconnect
Hoping to find a true sense of meaning in other things

Yet as long as we seek fulfillment
Based from a sense of self

We will remain divided
Within ourselves.

So what are we
If not ourselves?

Free

68

The Law of Attraction is based on
Some situation holding a key to what we need to learn

Hence karma is not quid pro quo
Based on some abstract notion of right and wrong

It is instead a Ping-Pong game that continues
As long as we are willing to volley what is served

The object then is not to win
But to stop playing once we understand

And create a new game of our own

69

People misunderstand the Tao
Much as they do Love

Mistaking the idea of Unity
With a single point of view

Or the idea of Love
With that special someone

Yet neither the Tao nor Love
Are about one way

Both are formless in order to nurture
Each thing on its own unique path

If we try to possess this formlessness
All we will find

Are things that must die

70

We have no higher or lower self
Just freedom or attachment to the material world

Hence what we "struggle" with
Is what we won't let go

Making the true problem
What we get used to.

Therefore, when we try to circumvent
The uncertainty of change

Freedom becomes our greatest fear
And evil the desire for convenience

This is why the Tao is not really hidden wisdom
If we are avoiding it.

71

What are the sounds of wind and rain?

Moving in the heavens, the wind is silent,
Only to be heard when it meets resistance

As it shakes the trees
Or fills our ears

Falling from the heavens, rain is also silent,
Only to be heard when it meets resistance

As it hits the roof
With its steady drumming

Both wind and rain come from silence
Yet are known by how they disturb the silence

Likewise, we come to know ourselves
Only by what we do,

Unaware of what we truly are.

72

Is it possible to plan for the future?

When we think we're ready
We're usually not

We can only be ready
For what we know

When we don't feel ready
We're prepared to learn

Yet we won't understand
Until we're transformed

夫

HEAVEN

73

Our thoughts behave
Like a flock of birds

When one arrives
A group soon forms

When one departs
The rest will follow

Thus we can observe
The nature of the mind

In the landscape of the Tao

74

Between unawareness
And thought

Thought
And action

Action
And result

Result
And responsibility

Curves a spiraling tornado
Whose center is the Tao

75

Between the mind and the world
Is the space of being

Yet between being and the mind
Is another space called consciousness

And between being and the world
Is yet another space called truth

Therefore the state of one's being
Either facilitates or muddles the connections

Between consciousness and the truth,
The mind and the world,

So that enlightenment must be clarity of being
Not a matter of consciousness or truth,

The mind or the world.

76

At what moment does a raindrop form?
From where does the wind originate?

Likewise, where does a thought begin
Before we know it is ours?

Can we perceive anything
Without falling into the trap of consciousness?

It is said that consciousness must stop
For the spirit to come alive

Consciousness stops when the mind is clear and empty
And we are not thinking about thinking

Like the shining of light
As it creates time and space

77

One cold day a powerful wind
Was blowing the trees back and forth.

Perched in one tree was a hawk
And in the same tree was a squirrel.

As the wind gusted violently
Both creatures struggled for balance

The hawk spread its wings and took off
But the squirrel was knocked from its branch

For a moment the small creature plummeted
But then grabbed another branch.

As the dark silhouette of the hawk faded in the
    distance,
The squirrel ran down the tree and into the woods

Such are the natures of the spirit and the mind
As they move with the Tao between heaven and earth.

78

Our mind is a flame
And our body is a candle

Yet what remains
When the fire and wax are done?

Such is the essence of the Tao

79

We know nothing of the summit
From the base of the mountain

Likewise, on attaining the peak
We will see everything below differently

Thus the true nature of the mountain
Is only revealed

By first climbing up
And then down its rocky slopes

We may also think of life
As a continuous series of mountains to scale

Yet if we live only for the view from mountain tops
Our joy will always be distant points on the horizon

On the other hand
If we can come to love climbing

Then our purpose
And that of every mountain

Are one

80

If existence is the eternal question
And the Tao the eternal lesson

Then every answer
We think we find

Creates another reason
For birth and death to exist

81

Cognition is the function of the mind
But its essence is emptiness

When we consciously think
Of this or that

We let ourselves be defined
By this or that

If our thoughts can instead be present
Yet formless like the darkness

Then a realization of the Tao can appear
Like the light at the end of a tunnel

道